LeRoy Neiman

LeROY NEIMAN AN AMERICAN IN PARIS

LeROY

AN AMERIC
UN AMÉRIC

HARRY N. ABRAMS,

NEIMAN

AN IN PARIS
AIN À PARIS

INC., PUBLISHERS

Editor:
Sharon AvRutick
Designers:
Samuel N. Antupit
and Liz Trovato

Library of Congress Cataloging-in-Publication Data
Neiman, LeRoy, 1927–
An American in Paris / LeRoy Neiman.
p. cm.
ISBN 0–8109–1950–8
1. Neiman, LeRoy, 1927– . 2. Paris (France) in art. 3. Paris (France)—Description and travel. I. Title
N6537.N39A4 1994
759.13—dc20 94–263

Published in 1994 by Harry N. Abrams, Incorporated, New York
A Times Mirror Company

Printed and bound in Italy

CONTENTS

Introduction 7

The Champs-Elysées 18

History 28

Chez Francis 34

Sur la Seine 40

Gloire de la France 44

July 14 46

Paris by Night 48

Paparazzi 52

Roland Garros 58

Sur le Pavé de Paris 60

Le Louvre 65

Fouquet's 66

Sketchbook 72

Waiters 96

Chefs 102

Haute Couture 110

Le Bois 114

Hippodromes 116

Le Tour de France 124

Un Café 128

A l'Opéra 130

The Ritz 134

Rive Gauche 138

Montparnasse 140

Montmartre 148

Service d'Honneur 150

TAITTINGE
PARFUM
Nº5
CHANEL
PARIS
COCO
CHANEL
LeRoy Neiman
'89-90

INTRODUCTION

Paris, la Ville-Lumière, is the city of pearly light and filtered sun. When the American first arrives in Paris, he feels his pulse increase. He is in a world capital dedicated to beauty above all else. Passionately, Paris presents the most magnificent, visually grand cityscape that anyone has ever set foot, hoof, or wheel upon. Its *très chic,* stunning women—the most elegant from around the world—are seen ceaselessly on parade with that certain Parisian whimsy on the fashionable, wide avenues. *Cherchez la femme! Vive Paris!*

Paris in the springtime: After the drizzle and the gray damp of winter, *le printemps* breaks, and glorious life blooms again on the terraces of the cafés. Just as crocuses pop up on park lawns and in flower boxes, the café exterior blooms with café goers. *Alors,* the sidewalk café, *c'est la joie de vivre!*

The first time I saw Paris and the Champs-Elysées was in late August 1944, during World War II. I was a GI cook with the American First Army during the Liberation of Paris. We had been on K rations since June 15 when my outfit, Battery D of the 461st AA Battalion, landed on Omaha Beach. After two months of grim, constant stop and go, never-ending combat conditions, and relentless fear and strain, we arrived with our guns at the outskirts of the city.

We held on the outside of Paris for about four days while the French, under Général Jacques Leclerc, liberated the city. Then our half-tracks rolled in to protect the Seine River bridges with our guns. Amid the exhilarating pandemonium of a heroes' welcome by the jubilant, flag-waving citizens of Paris throughout the streets and terraces strung with tricolor bunting, we encountered wine, women, and food—the likes of which we had never tasted in our young lives. It was beyond our wildest expectations. Unsophisticated and unmindful of the hardships and changes

VIVE DE GAULLE

La Liberation de Paris.

the populace had endured and was still going through (there was still sporadic fighting in the streets), we were "on the town."

In pairs or in groups, we GI's would independently venture out into the night on pleasure-seeking patrols and were not spared the dangers being experienced by the citizenry of Paris, such as being targeted by un-surrendered die-hard snipers holed up all over the place. You never knew when you were in the sights of *les boches'* guns, but there was no containing us. The contagious spirit of celebration prevailed.

The resilience of the people was unforgettable. The ambience of the cafés and nightclubs, and the flavor of the kitchens and *femmes* of Paris were as provoking then as they've continued to be to this day. Well armed with goodies—chocolate, gum, etc.—we introduced nylons to Paris as a bartering device. So the Parisiennes no longer had to paint lines down the back of their bare legs to simulate silk hosiery.

For centuries France's greatest writers—Proust, Baudelaire, Flaubert, Zola, Maupassant—had traipsed these very streets. It seemed every time you turned your head there was a street named in an author's honor: Avenue Victor-Hugo, Avenue Montaigne, Avenue Molière, Rue Balzac, Quai Voltaire.

Great restaurants such as Fouquet's, Lapérouse, La Tour d'Argent, Le Grand Véfour, and Maxim's were all as prominent then as they had been before the war and are still today.

But just to stand there on the cobblestones of the Champs-Elysées, the touchstone of so much of France's glorious past, was beyond comparison: Imagining the wedding party of Napoléon Bonaparte and his Austrian bride, Marie-Louise, in their coronation carriage followed by 100 other magnificent carriages in procession;

imagining Napoléon's funeral cortege solemnly proceeding down the Champs after his remains had lain in state under the Arc de Triomphe; imagining American General John J. Pershing prancing on horseback in tune with victorious World War I Yank and French soldiers.

Then on August 25, just a few hours earlier, Général de Gaulle walking triumphantly down the Champs, leading the victory parade en route to Notre-Dame. Thousands of Parisians exuberantly bouncing back, free after four years of strutting and swaggering Nazi rule, wildly cheering the general's every step.

Paris, with its tumultuous history, has been conquered by invaders and stormed by its own revolutionaries; it always rallies to reclaim its position as the world's urban capital of pleasure. What lore it holds!

When I first saw the Cathedral of Notre-Dame and the Paris Opera House, films I had seen as a kid in Saint Paul reeled off inside my head. Flashbacks to Lon Chaney as *The Phantom of the Opera* and Charles Laughton as Quasimodo in *The Hunchback of Notre Dame* . . . all pretty heady stuff for this Minnesota young blood. I was a part of history.

I didn't get back to Paris until 1960, when things were much calmer. I found myself once again seated, relaxed among the chairs and tables of the grand terrace of Fouquet's, sketching at my leisure. At about noon I settled down, a waiter briskly appeared, I put an apéritif behind my tie, lit my cigar, casually opened my sketchbook, and set to work.

During the early sixties I maintained studios in London and Paris, allotting considerable time to sketching this way in Paris sidewalk cafés. They became like my outdoor ateliers. I moved in the thick of famed café haunts on the Boulevard Saint-Germain, on the two *monts* (Martre *et* Parnasse), and in Les Halles, but I was always drawn back to the Champs. My allegiance to Fouquet's has never wavered, despite the attractions of other such establishments. (Holding strong, also on the Right Bank, is Chez Francis, which serves up a splendid view of the Eiffel Tower from its terrace.)

If Paris is the grand café of Europe, it is at Fouquet's that you feel its pulse. Fouquet's is what I call a pay-per-view café, the costly view being a vista of the upper portions of the Champs-Elysées, the "avenue of tourist dreams," topped by the Arc de Triomphe. The red awning of Fouquet's is a diadem, the badge of café royalty, a regal wrapping around the corner of the Champs-Elysées and the Avenue George-V.

HISTORY OF THE PARISIAN CAFÉ

The café, as we know it, goes back hundreds of years. The first restaurant as we know them today in Paris opened in the mid-18th century during the reign of Louis XV, and the French were quick to make coffeehouses into social and political gathering places. By 1789 the café, which served as a meeting place for agitators, was a central part of revolutionary life. As public discussion was censored, people depended on the word-of-mouth information that was available clandestinely in restaurants.

Coincidentally, in such public areas, the first real posters were circulated and posted by the monopoly of the church and the absolute authority of the crown—the church announcing the granting of indulgences, the state recruiting volunteers as well as making royal pronouncements.

The frequent upheavals in France in the 18th century gave rise to a proliferation of posters used as notices and proclamations. An example is the edict that was posted announcing the execution of Louis XVI at noon on Monday, the 21st of January 1793 in what was then known as the Place de la Révolution.

After the French Revolution chefs and stewards were freed from the king's and aristocrats' kitchens. As a result, unemployed chefs opened their own restaurants for the people, and the establishments flourished.

In the mid-1850s cafés prospered greatly. Restaurants and cafés pushed out onto the sidewalks, thanks to the spacious walkways provided by the newly created grand boulevards. *Bienvenue au sidewalk café!*

Posters were widely displayed. By the 1860s the artists established themselves, turning to the characteristic haunts of modern urban life, frequenting cafés and theaters.

By the 1860s and '70s the sidewalk café had become the perfect amenity—a fixture for a graceful society. Conversation found its perfection at table with profundity and reason in vogue.

The cafés' interiors were brilliant and mirror clad. From the terrace, colorful *affiches* announcing scientific, art, and entertainment events could be seen. Posters pictorialized the streets, being displayed everywhere there was traffic.

In Puccini's opera *La Bohème,* the Café Momus added to the scene. The café became the place to celebrate, to show off, to be a part of the street theater. It proved an irresistible lure, with cane chairs and tiny round marble tables beneath fluttering umbrellas or flapping overhanging awnings emblazoned with the establishment's name.

The boulevardier (a snob!) entered this milieu, as the flaneur was born. He frequented particular bars and cafés that he staked out, not mixing with strangers, thereby establishing a pattern of aloofness and propriety. Strangers would sit side by side without communicating, lounging and gazing.

By 1900 the sophistication of the sidewalk cafés' behavior patterns had progressed, along with the advancement of the poster. Posters' outdoor presence colorfully enhanced the grand avenues and boulevards of Paris.

Artists such as Toulouse-Lautrec, a café *habitué* himself, documented the end of the century with new-style original posters celebrating cabaret, music halls, and entertainers.

The tradition of the music-hall placards was carried on in the 1920s and '30s with snazzy avant-garde posters such as Paul Colin's Art Deco designs of Josephine Baker. Paris continued to set the high standard of quality by which posters are still measured.

Les Salons de Fouquet's, as it was known originally, dates back to 1899, opening during the Belle Epoque and the early years of the curvilinear forms of Art Nouveau. The outdoor table area is fronted today with a rotating *colonne* that flaunts advertisements making their pitch.

LEISURE

Early on I made the observation while sketching in public that people seated or standing for any length of time will always eventually resume the same position they were in when you commenced drawing them, no matter how often they've shifted about. Each of us has our own characteristic way of moving, taking into account an unseen ache, pain, or old injury.

The chair being occupied has something to say about movement and position. In the café the sitter is dictated to by surrounding objects like tables and umbrellas. Also, a café being a public situation, people are more often than not posing.

The café serves the artist's purposes by making its environs available for observation and to the process of drawing in the sketchbook. At a café, one is sedentary, which is ideal for either quick sketches or more prolonged renderings.

The artist feels obscure, even protected. There's no kibitzer standing over your shoulder. Each patron's space is their own. They are not to be bothered—to be observed, true, but no more than anyone else.

Sitting in a café sketching could be compared to sitting in a drawing class: Occupied chairs all around, most facing the same direction, in this case, the street. The waiter moves around among the seated just as the instructor does, bending over and taking an order in the same manner as a teacher gives a critique—confidential, one on one.

But the reality is that every seat is a ringside seat in the midst of a social menagerie. It's all part of the theater of the streets, providing animated candid studies of vital subject matter.

My thoughts will wander in the café setting while I'm working. The mind is challenged to relate and compare. I find myself pondering the great French painters from the past who worked in Paris, going back to Oudry, Watteau, and Fragonard up through Guys, Cézanne, Matisse, and Dufy, and to Robert Delaunay.

Manet, Monet, Renoir, Degas, and Braque all set the table for any future painter hooked on the tableau of the urban café.

The sidewalk café champions leisure and idleness. These philosophical arts presuppose tranquility and a contemplative attention to things entirely free from practical considerations. The French have always seemed to understand the synthesis of idleness and creativity.

One of the foundations of Western culture is leisure. We work in order to earn the leisure that is necessary to us, nourishing ourselves in festive companionship, restoring ourselves from our fatigue. Hence, the café—a respite from life's toil.

The Greeks considered toil to be necessary so that there can be leisure—which is, as Aristotle stated, "the centerpoint around which everything revolves."

Leisure draws its vitality from affirmation. Great imperishable intuitions come in these silent and receptive moments. Then the soul becomes aware of the forces that hold the world together.

Bravo, les cafés! Bravo, Paris . . . et merci!

AU PERE TRANQUILLE
AU PERE
TRANQUILLE

THE CHAMPS-ELYSÉES

The Champs-Elysées is the avenue of grand and historic occasions: Holiday parades, bridal parties, coronations, funeral corteges. In the 1960s President Charles de Gaulle pointed the way for re-establishing the glory of France, serving as a centerpiece in pomp-filled Champs-Elysées military parades (opposite). *Vive la France libre!*

LeRoy Neiman

PLACE DE GAULLE

In 1806 Napoléon decreed that a triumphal arch should be constructed here to commemorate the victories of his Grande Armée. The Arc de Triomphe was dedicated in 1836.

PLACE DE LA CONCORDE

The Place de la Concorde was originally named Place Louis XV (in 1754) and an equestrian statue of the king was erected in the center of the square. The statue was toppled in 1792 by revolutionaries, and the square was renamed Place de la Révolution. A guillotine replaced the monument and Louis XVI was beheaded there as he faced the Hôtel Crillon. The square was finally given its current name during the tenure of Louis-Philippe, King of the French, who ruled 1830–48.

THE OBELISK

In 1836 the guillotine was replaced by the 3300-year-old obelisk from the temple at Luxor. Gushing fountains play on either side of the Place de la Concorde centerpiece. In the middle distance, the red awning fronting Maxim's on the Rue Royale is visible (opposite above). *Les illuminations* at night (opposite below).

THE MARLY HORSES

The Place de la Concorde's oval framed by relentless, zany traffic (above). The entrance to the Champs-Elysées is marked by the Marly Horses, two rearing equestrian sculptures by Guillaume Coustou, which were installed in 1795.

LeRoy Neiman
72

The Champs-Elysées, *la Voie Triomphale,* where Parisians are as enchanted as tourists.

HISTORY

THE CATHEDRAL
OF NOTRE-DAME DE PARIS

The spiritual heart of the city, where Louis XVI and Marie-Antoinette attended a low mass on their first official visit to the capital on June 8, 1773, where Napoléon's spectacular coronation was solemnized on December 2, 1804, and where de Gaulle led a victorious parade from the Champs-Elysées for the Liberation Te Deum on August 26, 1944.

LOUIS XVI

Louis XVI, powdered and powerful, with his royal air of condescending superiority and patronizing disdain, could well have set the tone for the snobby maître d'hôtel in modern haute-cuisine French restaurants. But he's also remembered for the dignity he showed at his trial and his courage at the guillotine, proclaiming, "I die innocent . . . may my blood consolidate the happiness of France." What's more, he did support the Americans in their revolution.

NAPOLÉON BONAPARTE

The emperor, on the day of his marriage to Marie-Louise of Austria, offered a generous dowry to 6000 young women who would on the same day marry a soldier in his army who was of established bravery and good conduct.

GÉNÉRAL DE GAULLE

Charles de Gaulle, president of France (1958–69), standing erect and tall, as if he had swallowed his umbrella (as the French would put it), a great world leader of his time.

BALENC
Rolls Pall Mall tourer (american built)

AVENUE GEORGE-V

At the Place de l'Alma, south of the Champs-Elysées, two distinctive avenues, the Avenue George-V and the Avenue Montaigne—each only about a half-mile long—emanate from the terrace of Chez Francis and fork out to terminate at the Champs-Elysées.

Une journée agréable—lunch at Chez Francis.

chez francis

Une nuit d'excès—dining alfresco on the Chez Francis terrace.

TAXIS

AVENUE MONTAIGNE

The Avenue Montaigne is named after Michel de Montaigne, the immortal essayist called "the wisest Frenchman who ever existed." Its point of exit is the fountains at the Rond-Point.

DANS LA NUIT BLEUE

The fountains at the Rond-Point aglow, with the lights of the Arc de Triomphe shimmering in the distance.

SUR LA SEINE

Romantic views of the Eiffel Tower, as seen from the ornate single-span Alexander III bridge.

GLOIRE DE LA FRANCE

Le Petit Palais: Check out its portal sculpture for its class-A bang-up job of heroic pride and national glorification (above). The Arc de Triomphe du Carrousel was erected in the Place du Carrousel in 1806 to celebrate Napoléon's victories. Raffet's battlefield drawing of Napoléon serves as the model for my charcoal rendering (right).

JULY 14

LA FÊTE NATIONALE

Tricolors celebrating Bastille Day, and traffic along the tree-lined Champs up to the Arc.

PARIS BY NIGHT

LA REVUE DU LIDO

A flossy, feathery, frothy fandango: *Pas mal!*

G I R L S - G I R L S - G I R L S !

Crazy Horse Saloon: Striptease *à la française* (top). Backstage at the Lido (above left).
Sketching in the valley of Amazons: Lido dancers' dressing room in 1960 (above).

HOMAGE TO FRAGONARD

Folies Bergères: 1983 showgirl swinging out over the audience. A look back to Fragonard's romantic painting *The Swing* (c. 1766). Will she kick off a slipper?

Wallie

PAPARAZZI

Named after a photographer in Fellini's 1960 film *La Dolce Vita,* paparazzi came into notoriety and caught on in Paris in the early sixties as the craze to take candid photographs of celebrities for publication exploded. This 1970 wash drawing depicts three couples: The Duke and Duchess of Windsor, His Serene Highness Prince Rainier of Monaco and Her Serene Highness Princess Grace, and Aristotle and Jacqueline Onassis—all harassed constantly by paparazzi. The idea here was that the escorts always seem annoyed, and the ladies don't seem to mind, though of course this is not always the case. Apologies are extended in particular to Jackie for this.

Chez Maxim's, *un vendredi soir:* Writer Françoise Sagan at Maxim's, young, celebrated, and sought out, surrounded by allies and the lavish mirrors, filigree, and opulent Art Nouveau decor.

Possibly the all-time paparazzi preference: Brigitte Bardot at Chez Régine, the private club where she could sequester.

PAPARAZZI-PLAGUED PERSONAGES

Rudolph Nureyev (above left) defected to the West in 1961 and became an instant focus. He made his final appearance on stage with the Paris Opera Ballet in 1992, pursued all the while. Alain Prost (left), France's Formula One auto-racing champion, always fair game when on foot in Paris. An early target: Polo-playing playboy Porfirio Rubirosa at Bagatelle with fellow player, restaurateur Claude Terrail (above).

L E S   C A V E S   D E   P A R I S

The Club Saint-Germain, a popular pre-disco club in the sixties: A *cave* on the Rue Saint-Benoît, with its *noceurs* dancing to live jazz (above).

Tous les soirs at Régine's cellar disco (left). The twist craze held sway into the wee hours with Régine herself frequently providing the eurythmics on the dance floor while paparazzi noctambulists camped outside the *boîte*.

ROLAND GARROS

Paparazzi favorite: A flashy, gritty Yannick Noah was magnificent in his dramatic 1983 French Open win on the red clay (*terre battue*) at the Stade Roland Garros.

SUR LE PAVÉ DE PARIS

LeRoy Neiman
Paris '90

Le Bristol Paris
112, rue du Faubourg Saint-Honoré
Paris 84
LeRoy Neiman

un Parigot '62
LeRoy Neiman
Deux-Chevaux

LE COLISÉE

A prominent fixture on the Champs-Elysées, notorious all through the 1941–44 occupation. Could that possibly be Maupassant's character Monsieur Parent re-reading his newspaper?

LA BOURSE DU COMMERCE (1765)

1980 view of the floor of the Bourse de Paris, a distinctive gambling layout with the *corbeille,* a circular grated space surrounded by stockbrokers.

TWO AMERICANS IN PARIS

1960: *Écrivains* of different persuasions who found Paris agreeable—journalist Art Buchwald at the *Herald Tribune* meeting a deadline with wit, and novelist James Baldwin probably pondering *Another Country* or *The Fire Next Time.*

LE LOUVRE

The Musée du Louvre courtyard (top and above right). *La Victoire de Samothrace* (190 BC): As a salute to the land of *l'art du baise-main,* my *croquis marginal* of *Winged Victory*'s right hand remnants in a case next to the statue (above left).

Fouquet's

At Fouquet's on a balmy day the terrace is brisk and bustling.

LE PARIS
TAXIS
935 GXT 75

LE FIGARO
LeRoy Neiman 91-92

L'Heure de l'Apéritif. This 8 × 10 canvas was exhibited at the Grand Palais in the 1992 Salon d'Automne. Overleaf: Two details of this painting.

TAXIS

AU
BAL
NEGRE
DES
CHAMPS

PEUGEOT
les feuilles
CAFE GEORGE V
un motard

SKETCHBOOK

These and the following pages are from a sketchbook I worked in at my table at Fouquet's in 1991 and '92.

from Fouquets to the Arc
is the TWA building the
ornate Credit Commercial
Francais building, Air France
and Le Drug Store
LUX
SUN
TWA
Inès
Liaison – Building a
in cooker – a thickening, as of

GEORGE V
L'ambiance Parisienne

Footsie

hou-la-
Caprices et Frivolités de Pa

TAXI
Two kinds of people
study the posted exterior menu
one for palate preference
the other for prices
Everyday
Paris holds the center of
the European stage.

MERCEDES-BENZ
COGNAC
CAMUS
NAPOLEON
NORMANDY
MOULIN ROUGE
Paris
LIDO
que devenez-vous?
Laisse-moi tranquille
116 BIS CHAMPS ELYSEES
TOUT PARIS

à votre santé!

COGNAC
CAMUS
RADIO PHONE
NOUVELLE REVUE
LIDO
116 BIS CHAMPS ELYSEES (1) 45.63.11.61 ET AGENCES
BAL DU MOULIN ROUGE
FORMIDABLE
20 h Dîner dansant, Champagne et Revue 570 F
22 h et 0 h. Champagne et Revue 395 F
PRIX NETS - SERVICE COMPRIS
LA REVUE DU CENTENAIRE
Voilà!
Street Sweeper
no more blue coveralls
and twig and branch
brooms.
now green clad with
green plastic brooms

BUREAU DE POST
CHAMPS-ELYSEES
AVENUE
GEORGE V
AVENUE
DES
CHAMPS-ELYSEES
MERCI
- donnez-moi aussi
votre numéro
de téléphone !

– mes hommages,
Madame – – –

CASINO DE PARIS
JOSEPHINE
BAL NEGRE

OLYMPUS
TOSHI
VERNET
Quelques Aspects
de la vie de Paris

AVE
GEORGE V
AVE
des
Champs Elysées
Le dernier Tango à Paris

tango

GEORGE V
T'AS DE BEAUX YEUX, TU SAIS...

VERNET

J'ai deux amours,
mon pays et Paris

Brigitte et Françoise

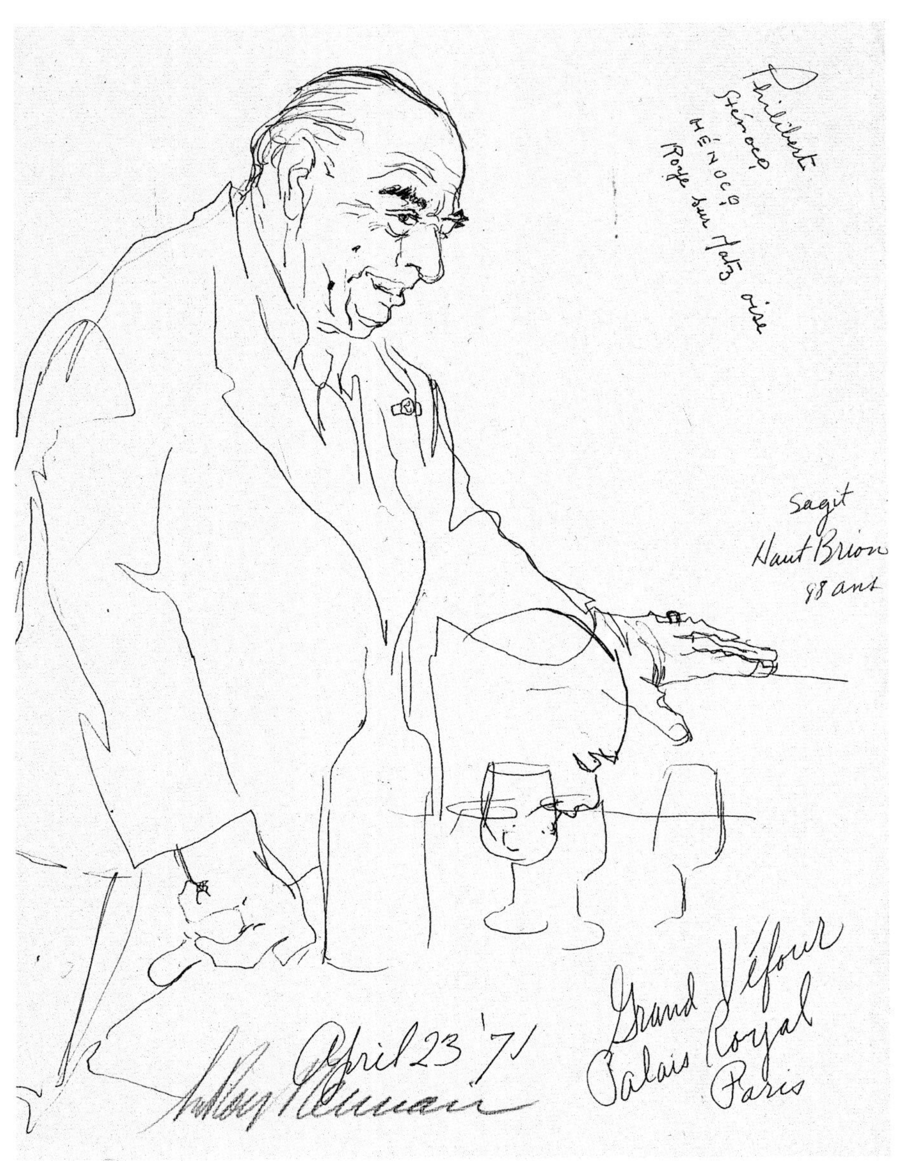
Haut Brion
April 23 '71
Grand Véfour
Palais Royal
Paris

RESTAURANT
51, Quai des Grands Augustins, PARIS. Tél. 326·68·04
R.C. Seine 60 A 23.173
TOPOLINSKI Ppre
Julian
15 ans a
waiter
'74
Lapérouse

SORTIE
L'addition
Paris
'74

WAITERS

THE DANCE OF THE *GARÇON*

The balletic balancer of trays, plates, bottles, cups, and glasses; rearranger of tables and chairs; deft decapper of soft drinks, beers, mineral waters; smooth uncorker of wines; muffler of popping champagne corks; pourer of coffee, tea, hot chocolate, and liquor; brisk at tearing checks, collecting money, making change, scooping up tips. You can depend on the Parisian waiter to be impeccably clean, efficient, impatient, and swift, moving economically on his toes as well as quick with a snappy comeback, whatever the tongue. He is never without the reliable white towel on his arm as he pirouettes and arabesques to the choreography of the café. Waitering is actually a service occupation: The *garçon* shows the competence and integrity of a specialist, maintaining detachment while meeting the patrons' every need. On your first visit, you pick your own table and are served. Second visit, your waiter recognizes you. Third visit, it is your table. Your fourth visit, he'll ask you if you're having the usual.

LeRoy Neiman Paris

LeRoy Neiman
Paris

the Singing Waiters

La Marseillaise

Allons enfants de la patrie!
Le Jour de gloire est arrivé!
Contre nous de la tyrannie
L'étendard sanglant est levé!
L'étendard sanglant est levé.
Entendez-vous, dans les cam
Mugir ces féroces soldats:
Ils viennent jusque
Egorger nos fils, nos
Aux armes! citoyens
Marchons! Marchons
Abreuve nos sillons

street troubador
a reimbodiment of the personification
of La Marseillaise on the bar relief
of the Arc de Triumph

gnes,
ans nos bras
ompagnes!
ormez vos bataillons!
u'un sang impur
Ye sons of France!
Awake to Glory!
Hark, hark, what myriads bid you rise:
Your children, wives and grandsires hoary,
Behold their tears and hear their cries!
Behold their tears and hear their cries!
Shall hateful tyrants mischief breeding
With hireling hosts,
a ruffian band, Affright and desolate the land, While
peace and liberty lie bleeding!
To Arms, to Arms, ye brave! Th'avenging sword unsheathe!
March on! March on! All hearts resolved
On Victory or death!
Shelley
LeRoy Neiman Paris

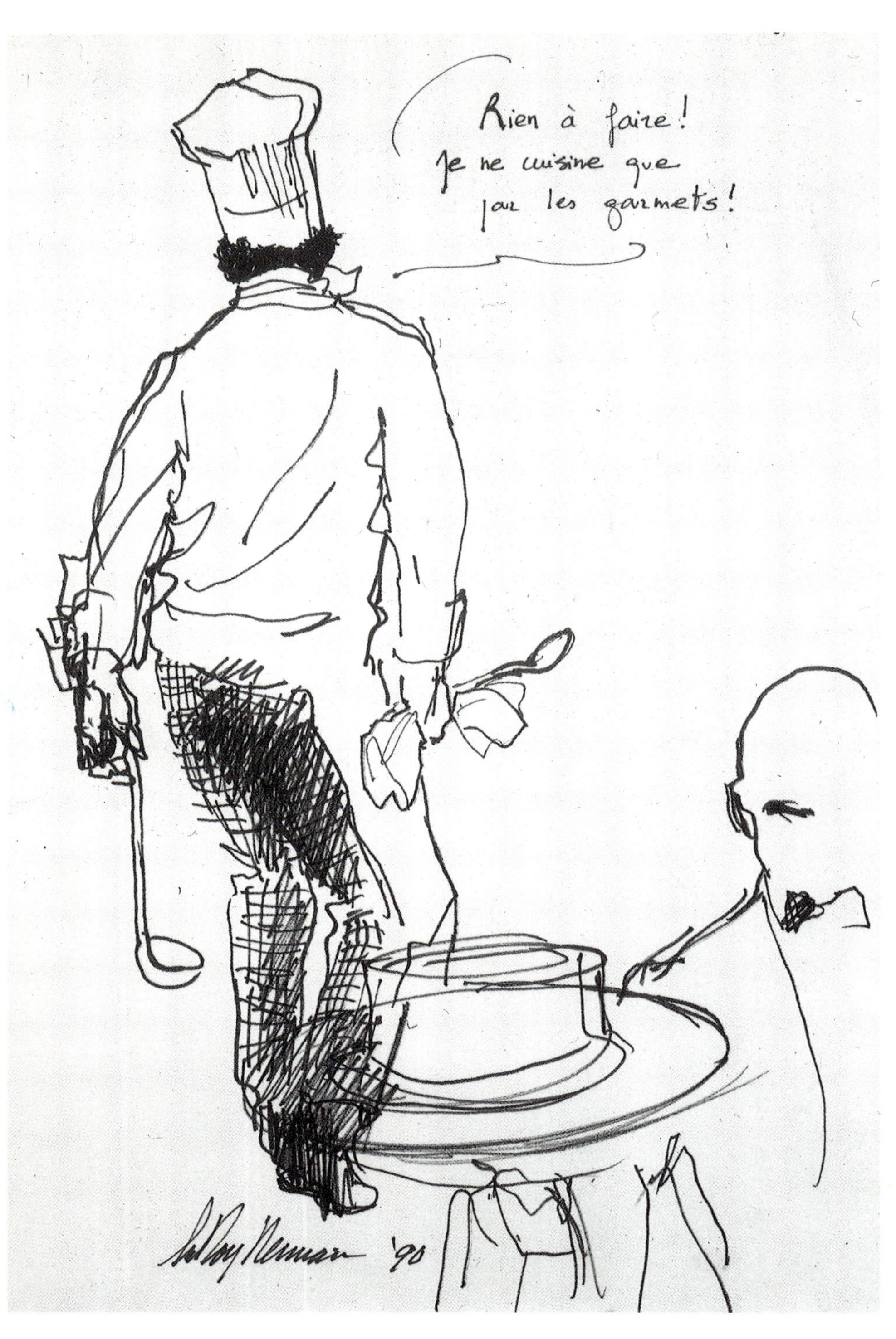

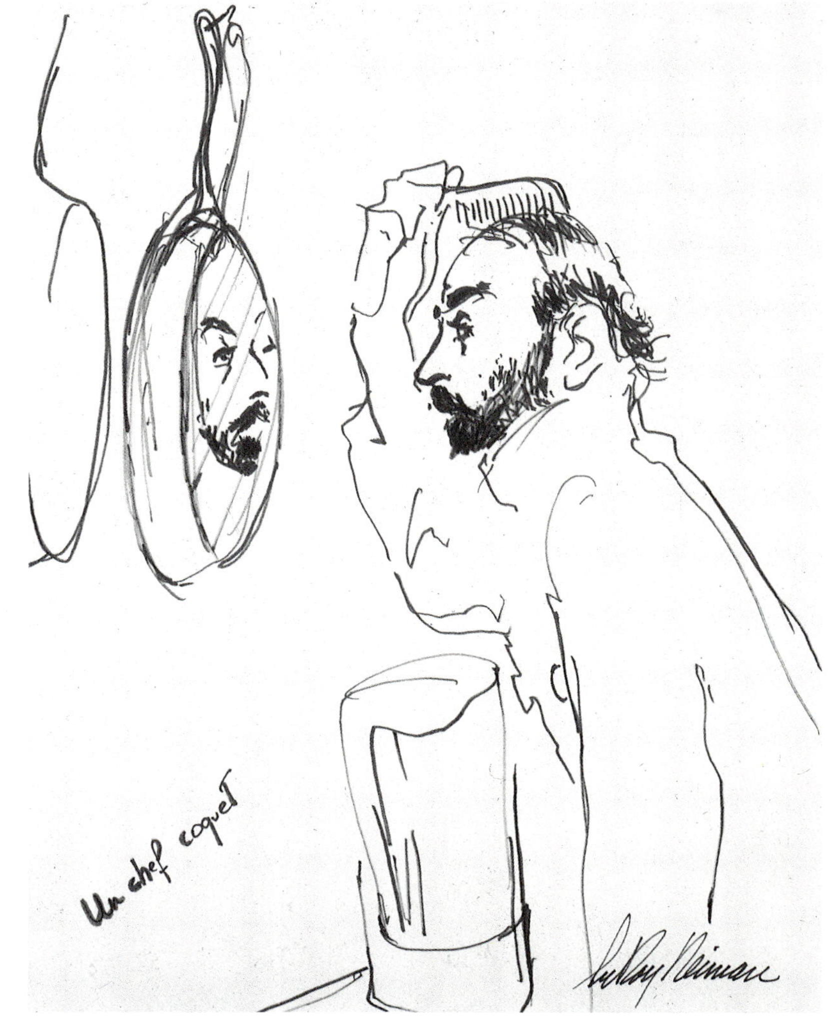

With Guy Martin in the Grand Véfour kitchen.

CHEFS

Born to cook, chefs can aspire to greatness because their art allows for just that in both creativity and dedication. In starched toques, they skillfully convert raw materials into appetite-pleasing digestibles, to the delight of the discriminating Parisian palate. Though impassioned, the *chef-coq* is constantly devising new recipes and menus with up-to-the-minute knowledge of nutrition and food chemistry. The *chef de cuisine* translates meat, fish, and game into dishes such as *Emincé de Boeuf à l'Echalotte, Filets de Sole en Papillotes, Crépinette de Canard à l'Orange,* and *Coq au Vin Pommes Landaises. A table, les gastronomes!*

The chef, *ce gros bonnet,* making a celebrity appearance in the dining room—an additional entrée for the gourmets.

CHATEAU
LYNCH-BAGES
PAUILLAC
ST EMILION
1957
CHATEAU
LA GAFFELIERE NAUDES
SAINT-EMILION
1959
PontLeRoy
CHATEAU NENIN
POMEROL
Puligny-Mont
SAINT-GEORGES
1955
Vin Rosé
Pétoulet
CHATEAU
GRAND-PUY DUCASSE
1959
PAUILLAC
MARGAUX
NUITS-LES-DIDIER
CLOS des CITEAUX
POMMARD
GRANDS CRU
1961
Moulin à Vent
CARQUELIN
Héritiers Crozet
DOMAINE
DE
LA CROIX
CHATEAU
LYNCH-BAGES
ROQUEFORT
SAUTERNES
CHATEAU
HAUT-BRION
PIPER
BEURRE
CHATEAU
Batailley

LE GRAND VÉFOUR

In the gardens of the Palais-Royal on July 12, 1789, standing on a café tabletop, Camille Desmoulins delivered his inflamed quavering "To Arms!" speech that kicked off the charge and fall of the Bastille on the 14th. Today, as it was then, on one corner of the elegant arcaded Palais-Royal quadrangle is the Comédie-Française, and on another, the gemlike, enchanting restaurant Le Grand Véfour. Le Véfour, which at the time of the Revolution was named Le Café de Chartres (the name is still etched in the window), is one of the great tables of the capital. The allegorical paintings on silk, mirrored walls, and ornate gilded woodwork of this 18th-century jewel dramatize the dining rooms' intimate sumptuousness. The gold trim throughout served originally to add additional brilliant light and glitter during the candle-chandelier years. The plush, wine-red velvet banquettes bear the nameplates of distinguished frequenters over the centuries, from Fragonard and Voltaire to Colette and Maria Callas.

A supposed gastronomic gathering at Le Grand Véfour. From the left: Victor Hugo, present director Jean Taittinger (standing), Alexandre Dumas, Colette, and Théophile Gautier; facing them are George Sand and Louis-Philippe; and Jean Cocteau and Honoré de Balzac are seated at the lower right.

LeRoy Neiman
Paris '93

RESTAURANT TAILLEVENT

Crème de la crème of gastronomy: A monument to the pleasures of the table with its subdued, classic dining rooms. The wine lists thirty years apart attest to Taillevent's claim of having the finest cellar in Paris—some 250,000 bottles.

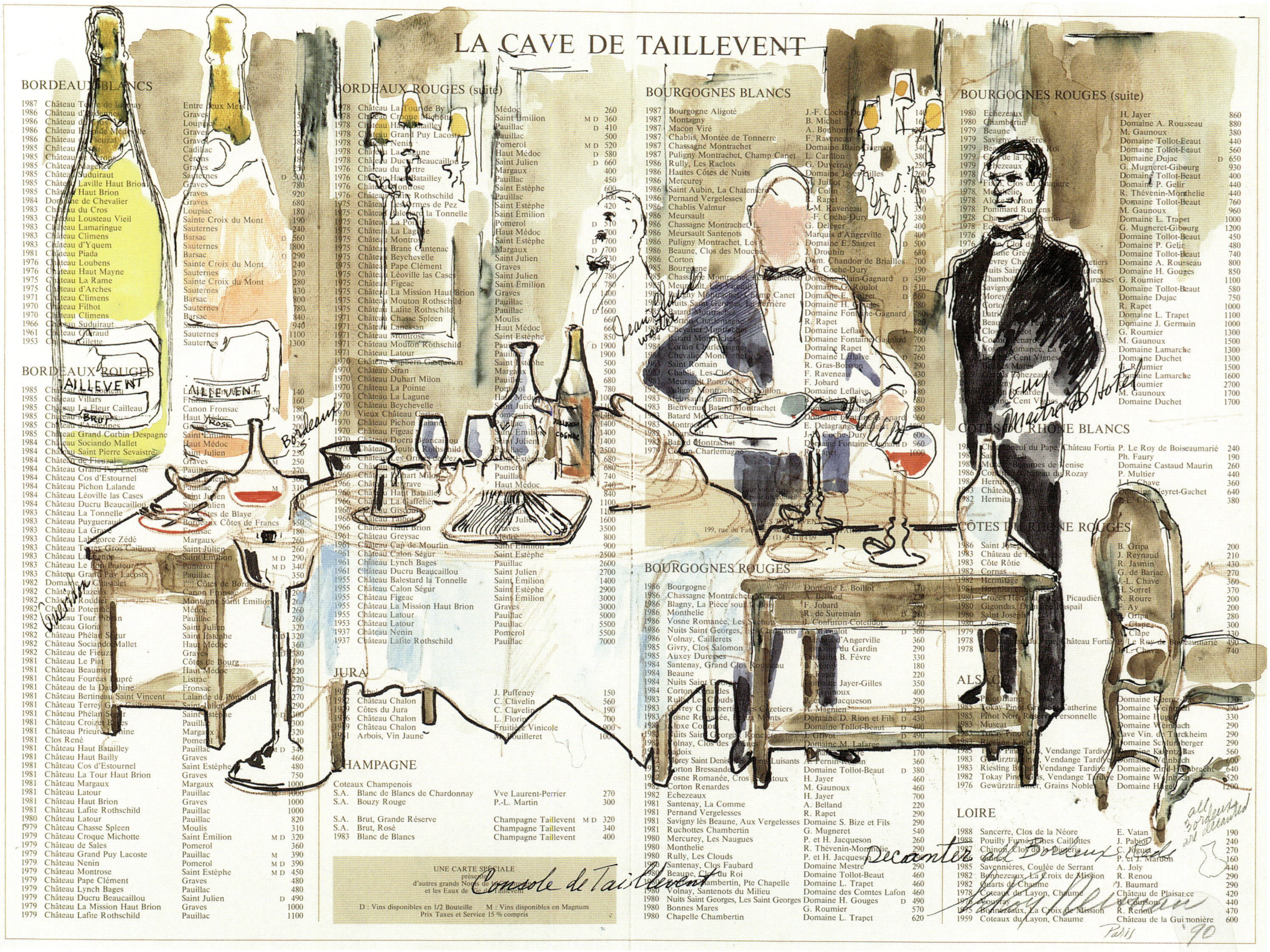

LA CAVE DE TAILLEVENT
BORDEAUX BLANCS
BORDEAUX ROUGES (suite)
BOURGOGNES BLANCS
BOURGOGNES ROUGES (suite)
BORDEAUX ROUGES
TAILLEVENT
BRUT
ROSE
Bordeaux
JURA
CHAMPAGNE
BOURGOGNES ROUGES
COTES DU RHONE BLANCS
COTES DU RHONE ROUGES
ALSACE
LOIRE
UNE CARTE SPECIALE
D : Vins disponibles en 1/2 Bouteille M : Vins disponibles en Magnum
Prix Taxes et Service 15 % compris
Console de Taillevent
Decanter
Maître d'Hôtel
all Bordeaux are decanted
Paris '90

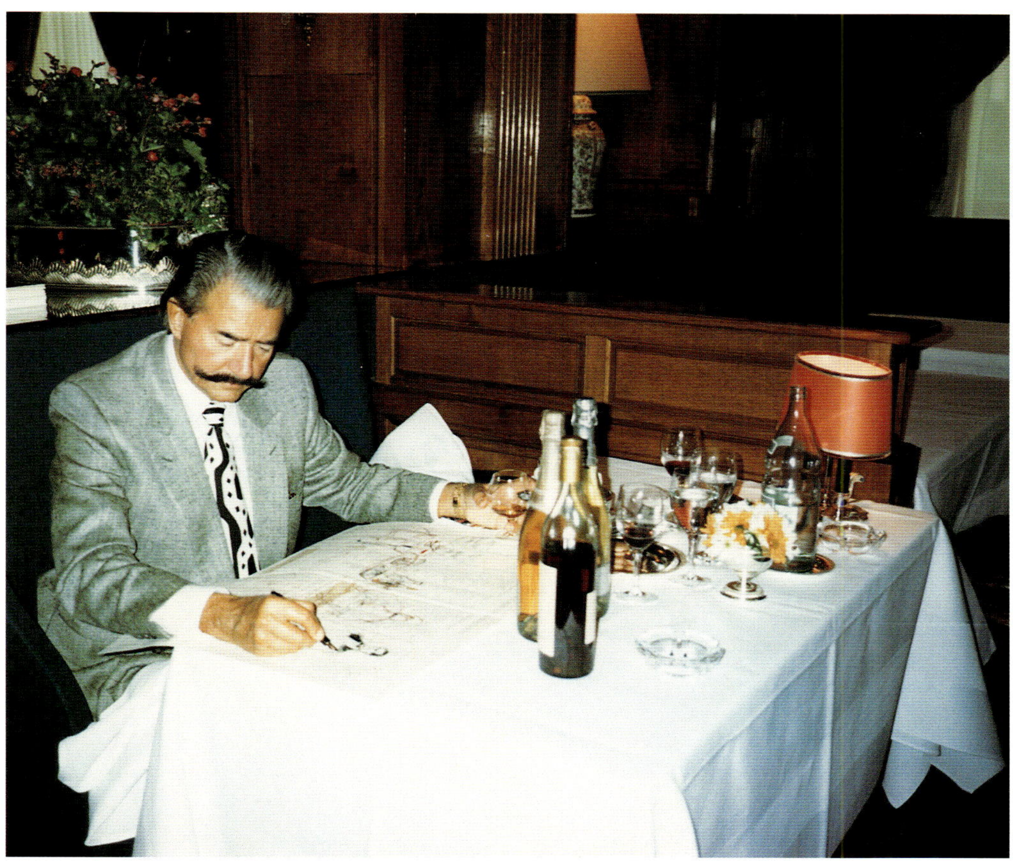

Proving that the artist doesn't always work best on an empty stomach . . . at a Taillevent table.

Mitterrand
Andre Leon Talley
Princess of Wales
Pamela Harriman
Tatiana

HAUTE COUTURE

Défilé of super-mannequins sashaying under the Carrousel on the runways of the Carrousel du Louvre.

Upholstering models in the atelier. The art of haute couture belongs to the French.

LE BOIS

BOIS DE BOULOGNE

Luncheon salad in the Bois in the open, 1980, more than a century after Manet painted his controversial wooded picnic scene, *Le Déjeuner sur l'herbe.*

HIPPODROMES

LONGCHAMP

Where horses run on the grass in the Bois de Boulogne. The paddock, where Raoul Dufy forever left his mark on French racing art. As well as the magnificent thoroughbred, the class of the gathering is the impetuous yet imperturbable preening Gallic jockey.

LeRoy Neiman
Jockeys entering paddock
at Longchamps
1960

Paddock at Longchamp
LeRoy Neiman '62

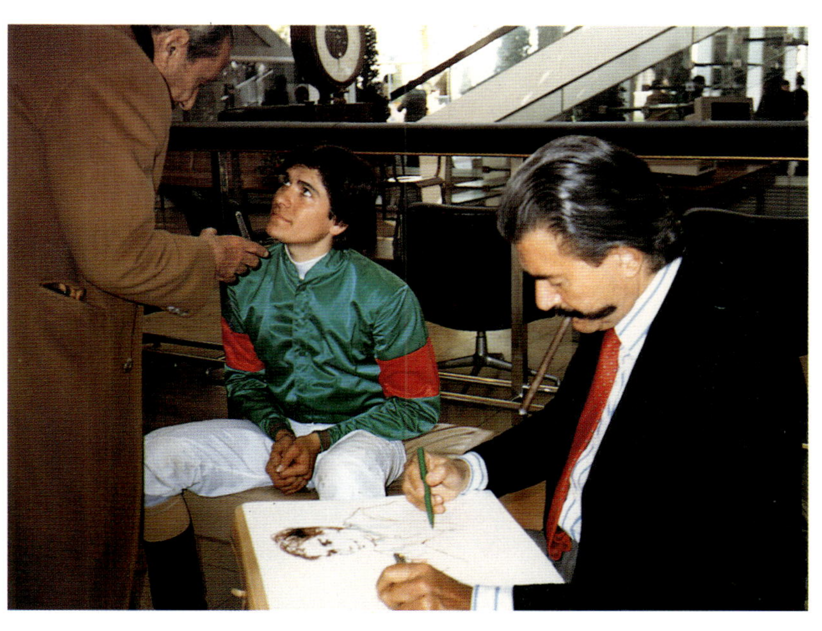

Sketching the American jockey Cash Asmussen in the jockey room at Longchamp.

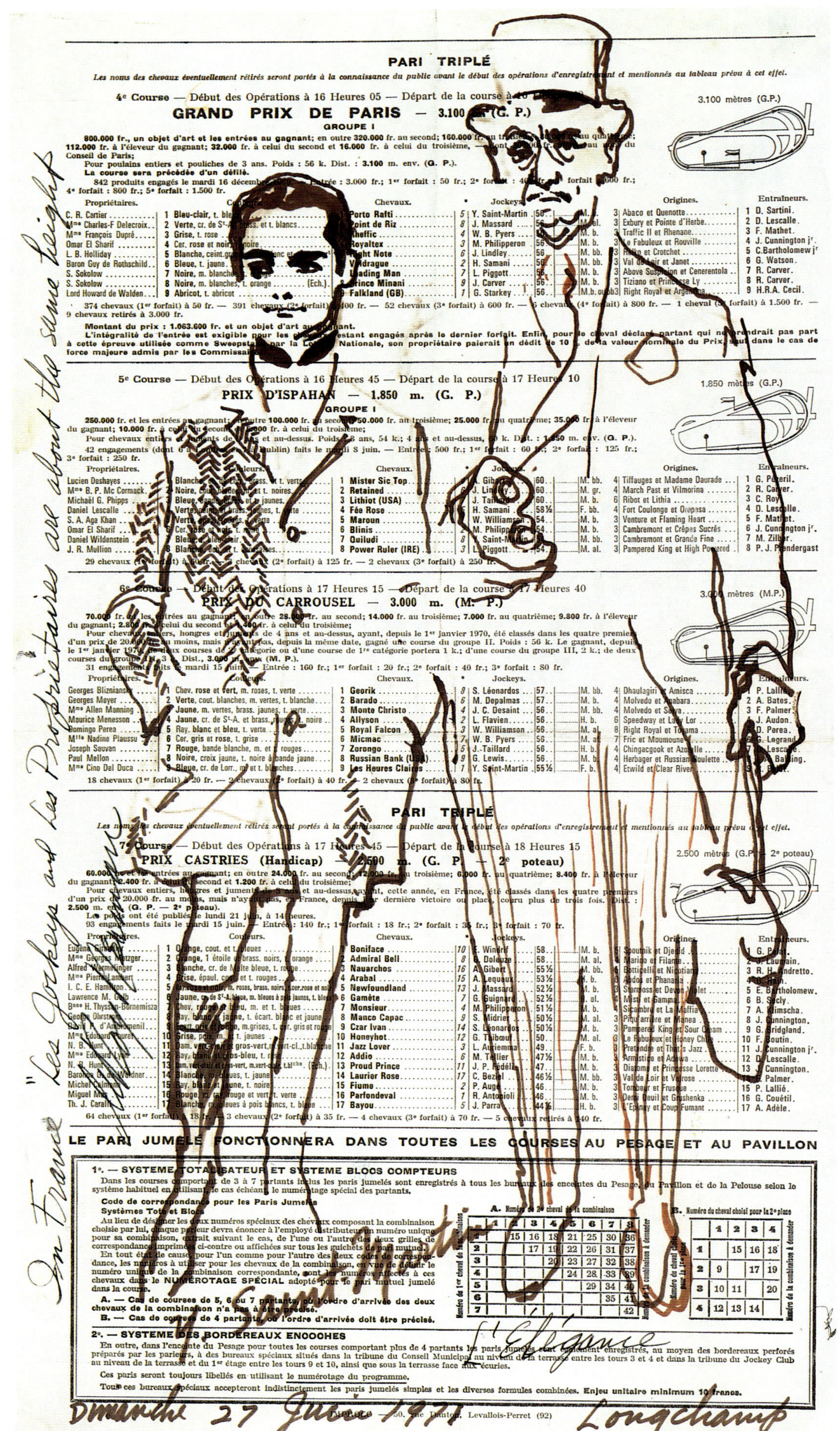

LE PRIX DE L'ARC DE TRIOMPHE (1993)

TEL PÈRE, TEL FILS

In the paddock at Longchamp on June 27, 1971: The legendary French jockey, number one of his time, Yves Saint-Martin (above), four-time winner of Europe's greatest horse race, Le Prix de l'Arc de Triomphe. In the same paddock at Longchamp on October 3, 1993, twenty-two years later: Eric Saint-Martin, son of Yves (right), on his first attempt in the Arc, riding number 12, a 25-to-1 long-shot filly named Urban Sea, won the Arc de Triomphe.

His comment: "It's good to keep it in the family."

The elite race goers who gathered in the paddock for the victory ceremonies following the stirring, historic win—special family triumph that it was—were indeed enthusiastic but true to form, *sans sentiment,* with the low-key hand-clapping and hand-shaking of good breeding. After all, the lineage was French.

LeRoy Neiman
E. SAINT-Martin
L'Arc de Triomph
Longchamp
Dimanch 3-10 98

Auteuil, the Bois steeplechase course, the incomparable water jump in front of the tribune.

Aristocratic polo on the same lawns of the Bois at Bagatelle.

WINNERS

Three yellow-shirted cyclists—Frenchmen Jacques Anquetil (above) and Bernard Hinault (right) and American Greg LeMond (opposite)—all of whom won the grueling Tour de France three times.

LE TOUR DE FRANCE

On slick, wet cobblestones the bikes turn into the Rue de Rivoli, heading for the finish at the Arc de Triomphe. The Jardin des Tuileries serves as a backdrop with the Eiffel Tower in the distance in this last stage of the Tour de France.

ON LOCATION

The balcony of the Hôtel Regina, Place des Pyramides, with a view of the gilded statue of Jeanne d'Arc below.

de la paix Café de la paix

UN CAFÉ

THE ART OF
CAFÉ SITTING

Café de la Paix, situated on the bustling Place de l'Opéra.

À L'OPÉRA

Reminiscent of Georges Seurat's conté drawing *Street Sweeper* (1887–88), the time-honored, ever-present *balayeur des rues* (over 4000 street sweepers attend Paris' 5000 streets every day) now wears green rather than the former accustomed *bleu de travail.*

LA FAÇADE DE L'OPÉRA GARNIER

Executed in keeping with Second Empire architecture, the Carpeaux sculpture *La Danse* adorning the front was controversial at its unveiling in 1869 and still maintains a presence today.

LE GRAND ESCALIER DE L'OPÉRA

The grandeur of the opera house interior, the setting of countless formal and official occasions.

THE RITZ

Take your Rolls to the Ritz. A pedigreed guest disembarking to check into the hotel. The tariff for a dog runs about $100 a day.

Sanctuary of *l'art de vivre*: The garden of the Ritz at lunchtime, overseen by the graceful recumbent stone sphinx with the body of a lion and the head and breast of a woman. Oscar Wilde wondered, "Who were her lovers?"

Expensive cars and people arriving at and departing from the Ritz.

LE RELAIS ODÉON

Latin Quarter hangout spilling out into the street, in keeping with the youthful, teeming environs of the Théâtre de l'Odéon and the Sorbonne.

RIVE GAUCHE

L E   Q U A I   D E   L A   T O U R N E L L E

A typical Quai café with an eye-level view of the buttresses and towers of Notre-Dame Cathedral, a presence that extends beyond the religious.

MONTPARNASSE

L A C O U P O L E

Energetic *Montparnienne* big and noisy illustrious bistro bastion, since the twenties a landmark, along with other legendary hangouts of artists such as the Select, the Dôme, and the Rotonde.

en montparnasse
LA COUPOLE
RESTAURANT_BRASSERIE
LA COUPOLE
102, BOULEVARD DU MONTPARNASSE (XIVe)
Fermeture le jeudi 14 Avril 1988. Réouverture en Décembre.
EN MONTPARNASSE
le 11 AVRIL 1988
FINES DE CLAIRES
SPECIALES
PLATES DE HOLLANDE
HORS D'OEUVRES
Bisque de Homard 32- Consommé chaud 19-
Soupe à l'Oignon gratinée (le soir) 30-
Escargots de Bourgogne la dz 76-
Saumon fumé artisanal, blinis à la crème 99-
Médaillon de Lotte 44
en gelée à la catalane
Quart de Poulet froid 45-
SPECIALITES
Cassoulet d'oie à la Castelnaudary 69-
Formidable choucroute paysanne
POISSONS
1/2 Langouste 115-
à la Parisienne
PLATS DU JOUR
STEAK TARTARE 75-
Pommes Frites
SAUMON FRAIS FROID AUX POINTES D'ASPERGES 84-
QUENELLES DE BROCHET SAUCE NANTUA 59-
SUPREME DE BARBUE AU SAFRAN 89,50
TRUITE AUX AMANDES 62-
MERLAN FRIT SAUCE TARTARE 55-
SOLE MEUNIERE 92-
GIGOT D'AGNEAU ROTI GRATIN DAUPHINOIS 79,50
TETE DE VEAU SAUCE VINAIGRETTE 67,50
CONFIT DE CANARD POMMES A L'AIL 74-
COEUR DE FILET DE BOEUF AU POIVRE 94-
GRILLADES
Châteaubriand sauce béarnaise 94-
Pied de Porc Pané 49,50
BRASSERIE LA COUPOLE
BAR AMERICAIN
DESSERTS
Soufflé au Grand Marnier (20mn) 42-
Salade de fruits au kirsch 33-
Entremet Citron avec son Coulis de Groseilles 32,50
Tarte au Citron 33-
Pruneaux d'Agen à l'Armagnac 28-
GLACES ET SORBETS
Domaine des Dreux
Appellation Sancerre Controlée
DISTRIBUE EN EXCLUSIVITE RICHARD
PIECE D'IDENTITE EXIGEE POUR TOUT PAIEMENT PAR CHEQUE
Café express et Décaféiné 8,50
SERVICE 15% COMPRIS

CINEMA
LIPP
LIPP
LIPP
LIPP

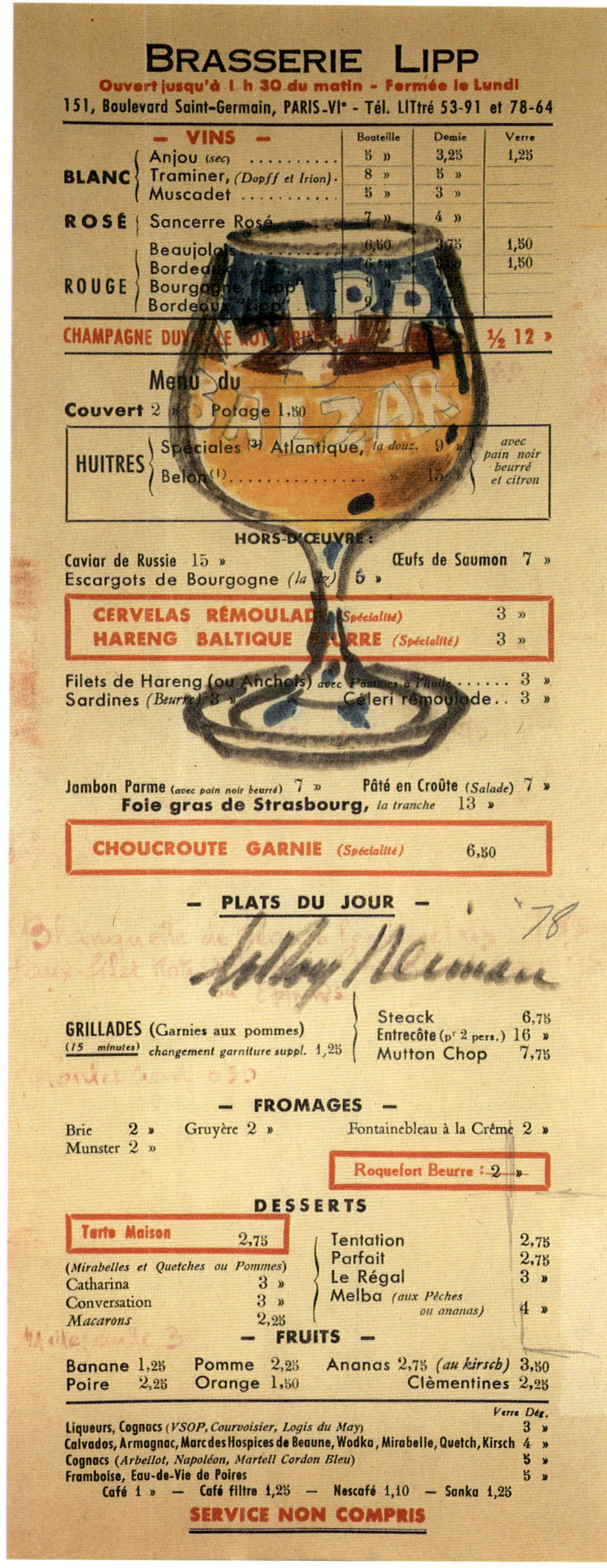

BRASSERIE LIPP

Ouvert jusqu'à 1 h 30 du matin - Fermée le Lundi

151, Boulevard Saint-Germain, PARIS-VIe - Tél. LITtré 53-91 et 78-64

— VINS —

		Bouteille	Demie	Verre
BLANC	Anjou *(sec)*	5 »	3,25	1,25
	Traminer, *(Dopff et Irion)*	8 »	5 »	
	Muscadet	5 »	3 »	
ROSÉ	Sancerre Rosé	7 »	4 »	
ROUGE	Beaujolais	6,50	3,75	1,50
	Bordeaux	[illegible]	[illegible]	1,50
	Bourgogne "Lipp"	9 »	[illegible]	
	Bordeaux "Lipp"	9 »	[illegible]	

CHAMPAGNE DU[illegible] ½ 12 »

Menu du

Couvert 2 » Potage 1,50

HUITRES { Spéciales (3) Atlantique, *la douz.* 9 » / Belon (1) ... 15 » } *avec pain noir beurré et citron*

HORS-D'ŒUVRE :

Caviar de Russie 15 » — Œufs de Saumon 7 »
Escargots de Bourgogne *(la dz)* 6 »

CERVELAS RÉMOULADE *(Spécialité)* 3 »
HARENG BALTIQUE BEURRE *(Spécialité)* 3 »

Filets de Hareng (ou Anchois) *avec Pommes à l'huile* ...... 3 »
Sardines *(Beurre)* 3 » — Céleri rémoulade .. 3 »

Jambon Parme *(avec pain noir beurré)* 7 » — Pâté en Croûte *(Salade)* 7 »
Foie gras de Strasbourg, *la tranche* 13 »

CHOUCROUTE GARNIE *(Spécialité)* 6,50

— PLATS DU JOUR —

GRILLADES (Garnies aux pommes)
(15 minutes) *changement garniture suppl.* 1,25
Steack 6,75
Entrecôte (pr 2 pers.) 16 »
Mutton Chop 7,75

— FROMAGES —

Brie 2 » — Gruyère 2 » — Fontainebleau à la Crême 2 »
Munster 2 »
Roquefort Beurre : 2 »

DESSERTS

Tarte Maison 2,75
(Mirabelles et Quetches ou Pommes)
Catharina 3 »
Conversation 3 »
Macarons 2,25
Tentation 2,75
Parfait 2,75
Le Régal 3 »
Melba *(aux Pêches ou ananas)* 4 »

— FRUITS —

Banane 1,25 — Pomme 2,25 — Ananas 2,75 *(au kirsch)* 3,50
Poire 2,25 — Orange 1,50 — Clèmentines 2,25

Verre Dég.
Liqueurs, Cognacs *(VSOP, Courvoisier, Logis du May)* 3 »
Calvados, Armagnac, Marc des Hospices de Beaune, Wodka, Mirabelle, Quetch, Kirsch 4 »
Cognacs *(Arbellot, Napoléon, Martell Cordon Bleu)* 5 »
Framboise, Eau-de-Vie de Poires 5 »
Café 1 » — Café filtre 1,25 — Nescafé 1,10 — Sanka 1,25

SERVICE NON COMPRIS

BRASSERIE LIPP

The patriarch of the three literary cafés on the Boulevard Saint-Germain—Lipp, Flore, and Deux Magots: Lipp is a cherished relic of Paris, a Left Bank institution, and a national monument. The long-white-aproned waiters are unmatchable throwbacks, and its time-honored denizens are irreplaceable.

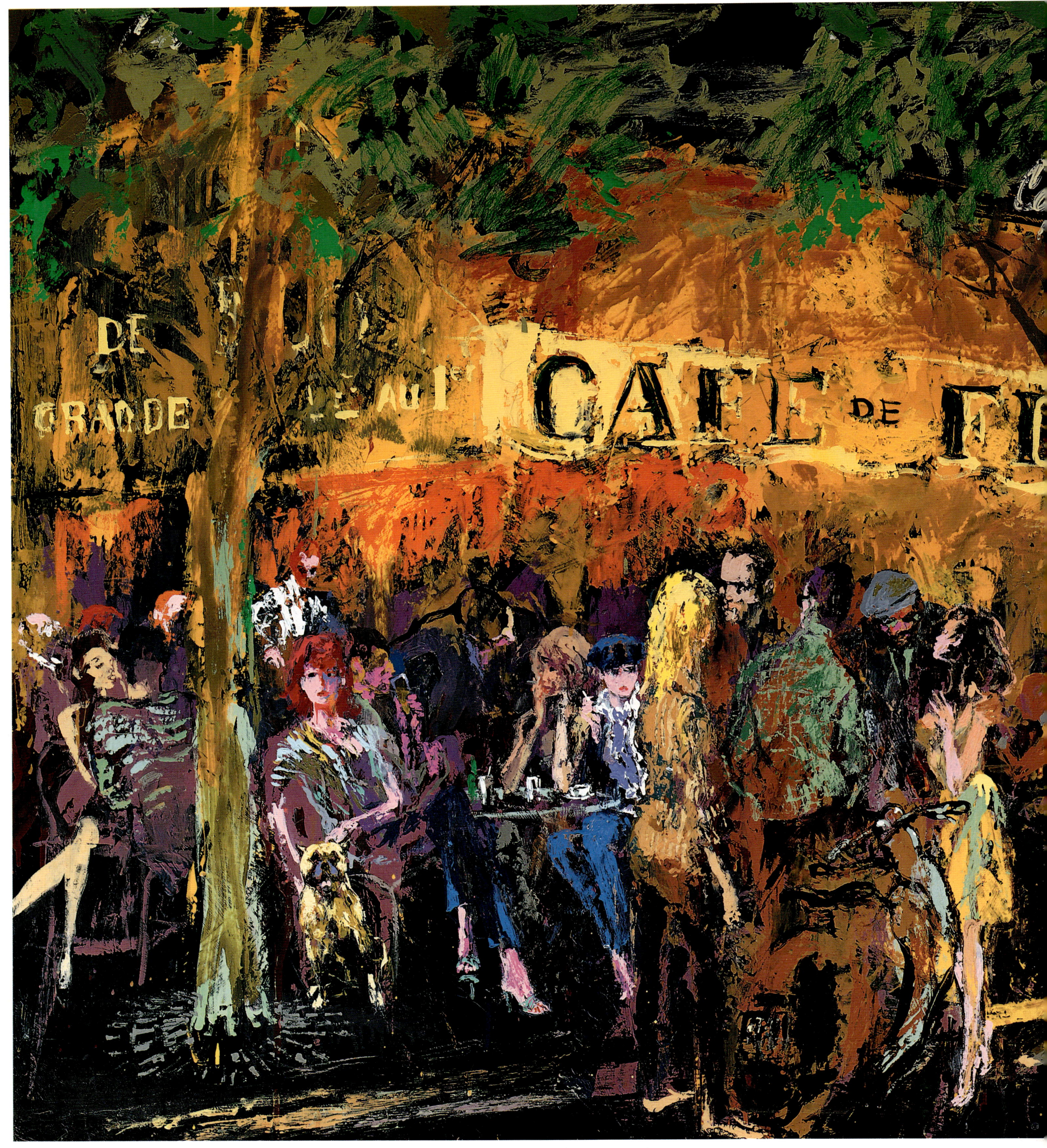
DE
GRANDE
CAFE DE

CAFÉ DE FLORE

Across the street the French reverence for words and writing is perpetuated by the twins Café de Flore and the Deux Magots, which share a stretch of sidewalk just yards apart, separated only by a bookstore. Both cafés occupy their own corners.

AUX DEUX MAGOTS

The endless passing parade of strollers along the boulevard peer into the sedentary gathering while those seated in turn curiously stare back out at them. The clientele seated on the Rue Bonaparte side face the ancient church of Saint-Germain-des-Prés.

Magots

MONTMARTRE

CANCAN

The exuberant rhythms of Offenbach, Cole Porter's *Can-Can,* and the red- and-orange-haired *cancaneuses* with their lace bloomers, garters, black stockings, and multiple petticoats exemplify the undimmed gaiety of the spirited cancan (this page). The Moulin Rouge (opposite) is another *monument historique* on the Place Blanche. The windmill sails revolve atop this cabaret just as they did back when beckoning to Toulouse-Lautrec.

ULIN ROUGE
BAL
DU
ROUGE
JANE
AVRIL
CYR
DANSE
TABA
LeRoy Neiman

SERVICE D'HONNEUR

On grand occasions the prestigious Garde Républicaine turns up in full historic regalia, helmeted and plumed, with salutes of upraised sabers.

THE CABIN OF THE CONCORDE
"THE WAY TO GO"

A characteristic French concept designed to provide swift transportation for travelers who just can't get to New York or Paris quickly enough.

UN CAFÉ FERMÉ

Tables and chairs rest before the arrival or after the departure of *les habitués.*

CREDITS

Editorial Assistants: Isabelle Balot-van Caloen and Lynn Quayle

PHOTOGRAPHS

Janet Byrne-Neiman 17; Brigitte Perron 127, 136;
Playboy Magazine 50; Lynn Quayle 41, 66, 109, 119, 145

GALERIE O. BOSC

6, Avenue Delcassé — PARIS VIII — Tél. BAL 47-43

LEROY NEIMAN

27 NOVEMBRE — 11 DECEMBRE 1962

Vernissage le Mardi 27 Novembre de 16 à 19 heures

BERNARD NEYROLLES — IMP. LESCARET, PARIS

Exposition particulière, 1962.

Exposition particulière, 1993.